MOANA
COLLECTION FOR YOUNG VOICES

TABLE OF CONTENTS

How Far I'll Go 2
Shiny 5
We Know The Way 11
Where You Are 13
You're Welcome 18

Characters and Artwork © Disney Enterprises, Inc.

For all works contained herein:
Unauthorized copying, arranging, adapting, recording, Internet posting, public performance, or other distribution of the printed music in this publication is an infringement of copyright. Infringers are liable under the law.

These arrangements are for concert use only. The use of costumes, choreography or other elements that evoke the story or characters of this musical work is prohibited.

Walt Disney Music Company
Wonderland Music Company, Inc.

DISTRIBUTED BY

7777 W. BLUEMOUND RD. P.O. BOX 13819 MILWAUKEE, WI 53213

In Australia Contact:
Hal Leonard Australia Pty. Ltd.
4 Lentara Court
Cheltenham, Victoria, 3192 Australia
Email: ausadmin@halleonard.com.au

Visit Hal Leonard Online at
www.halleonard.com

HOW FAR I'LL GO

Music and Lyrics by
LIN-MANUEL MIRANDA

Moderately (♩ = 80)

opt. Solo
mp

I've been star-ing at the edge of the wa-ter long as I can re-mem-ber, nev-er real-ly know-ing why.

I wish I could be the per-fect daugh-ter, but I come back to the wa-ter no mat-ter how hard I try. Ev-'ry turn I take, ev-'ry trail I track, ev-'ry path I make, ev-'ry road leads back to the place I know where I can-not go, where I long to be. See the

end Solo
All mf

© 2016 Walt Disney Music Company
All Rights Reserved. Used by Permission.

WE KNOW THE WAY

Music by OPETAIA FOA'I
Lyrics by OPETAIA FOA'I and
LIN-MANUEL MIRANDA

© 2016 Walt Disney Music Company
All Rights Reserved. Used by Permission.

*Tay fay-noo-ah tay mah-lee yay. Nah-yay koh hah-kee-lee-yah

YOU'RE WELCOME

Music and Lyrics by
LIN-MANUEL MIRANDA

© 2016 Walt Disney Music Company
All Rights Reserved. Used by Permission.

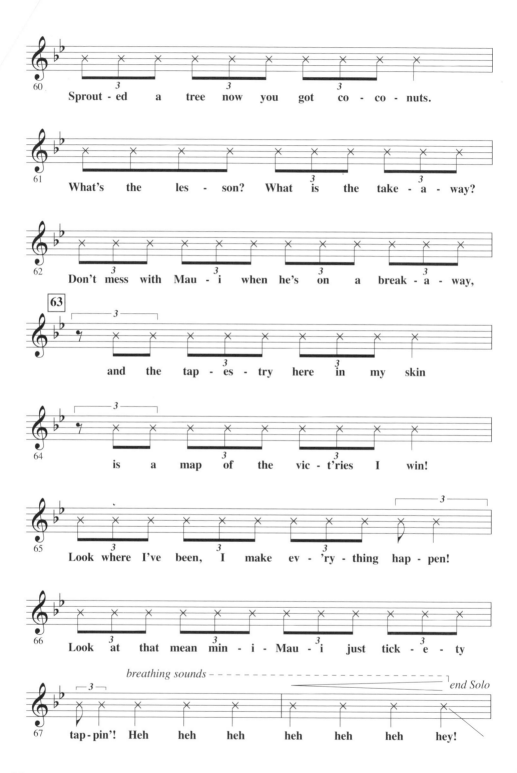